Kate

The story so far...

igloobooks

igloobooks

Published in 2013
by Igloo Books Ltd
Cottage Farm
Sywell
Northants
NN6 0BJ
www.igloobooks.com

Written by Helen Jaeger

All images featured in this book are courtesy of Getty Images © Getty Images

SHE001 0713
2 4 6 8 10 9 7 5 3 1
ISBN: 978-1-78197-385-1

Printed and manufactured in China

Contents

Catherine, Duchess of Cambridge and Prince William, Duke of Cambridge kiss on the balcony at Buckingham Palace on April 29, 2011 in London, England.

Introduction

Kate is the middle-class girl who married a prince - but the fairytale is even more impressive than that. In just one hundred years and three generations, Kate's family has moved from pits to palace.

Kate's family line through her mother's side of the family leads back to a coal-mining village in the North-East of England. Kate, who will be the future Queen Consort of England and mother of a monarch, comes from ancestors who lived in Hetton-le-Hole, County Durham. Even today, Kate has family in the area, including a cousin, who is a hairdresser. One of her mother's relations, James Harrison, was a coal miner in County Durham in 1819, the year that Queen Victoria was born. Other family members include a plasterer, general labourer and domestic servant.

The family fortunes began to change with Kate's grandmother, Elizabeth Temple. A formidable Northern lady, Elizabeth envisaged a better future for herself and her family. She believed that moving to London with her husband would secure that. Elizabeth and Thomas' daughter was Dorothy Harrison, who also inherited her mother's desire to better herself (she was even known affectionately as 'Lady Dorothy' to her relations, in recognition of her ambitions).

Dorothy, Kate's grandmother, married Ronald Goldsmith. Their daughter, Carole Elizabeth Goldsmith was born on 31st January 1955. Carole's father was then a builder and the family lived in a council flat in Southall, while Carole attended the local state school.

After leaving school, Carole worked as an air stewardess – a job considered glamorous in the 1970s. While in that job, Carole met and fell in love with Michael Middleton, Kate's father and they were married in 1980. Their first daughter, born in 1982, was Catherine Elizabeth Middleton, known as Kate.

Catherine, Duchess of Cambridge arrives at the Royal Albert Hall on May 11, 2012 in London, England.

Catherine, Duchess of Cambridge attends an official dinner hosted by
Malaysia's Head of State Sultan Abdul Halim Mu'adzam Shah of Kedah.

The Beginning

Birth

Kate Middleton was born 'Catherine Elizabeth Middleton' on the 9th January 1982 to Carole and Michael Middleton. It was a Saturday. Kate was born on the maternity ward at the Royal Berkshire Hospital, which is about a fifteen minute walk from the centre of Reading in Berkshire. She is the eldest of three siblings – her sister, Pippa, was born in September 1983 and her younger brother, James, was born in April 1987.

Kate was christened at the parish church of St Andrews, Bradfield, in Berkshire on June 20th 1982. The new family lived in a modest semi-detached house. Carole, her Mum, was a former air stewardess and Michael, her Dad, was at the time working for British Airways. Kate is six months older than Prince William.

Michael Middleton and Carole Middleton arrive at The Palladium Theatre on October 10, 2011 in London, England.

Kate Middleton aged three on a family holiday in the Lake District.

Kate Middleton with sister Pippa and Father Michael in Jerash, Jordan.

A general view of the ruins in Petra, Jordan.

Early Years

When Kate was very little, her parents, Michael and Carole Middleton both worked for British Airways. Michael was a manager and Carole a flight attendant. In May 1984, when Kate was just two years old, Michael was offered a posting to Amman, capital of Jordan. Carole was on extended leave with Kate's baby sister, Pippa, who had been born in September 1983 and was by then eight months.

During the week, Michael was very busy with work, so the family didn't have a very active social life. They were members of the British Embassy Club, where Michael would play tennis and they would visit Jordanian attractions, such as Petra, at the weekend.

The family lived in a two-storey rented villa close to a park and the nursery Kate attended. The nursery, called the 'Assahera' nursery, was one of the most expensive in the area with a fee of about one thousand US dollars a year. The nursery opened from Sunday to Thursday, the working week in the Middle East, with the daily session starting at 8am and finishing at 12.30pm. Usually it was Carole who picked her daughter up – but sometimes Michael would, too.

Kate was in a class of 12 children and the nursery looked after almost one hundred children aged between three and five years old. The nursery was international with children from various backgrounds, including Britain, Jordan, Japan, India, Indonesia and America. In the morning, the children were taught in both English and Arabic, learning popular nursery songs such as 'Incy Wincy Spider' in both languages, before separating into different classes. Religious teaching was also fully inclusive, with verses from the Quran taught, as well as events such as Christmas being celebrated.

At half past nine the children would sit down to a breakfast of hummus, cheese and labneh. They would feed rabbits and ducks, play in the sandpit and take part in creative activities. The family returned to the UK in September 1986, when Michael Middleton's posting came to an end. They settled in Berkshire and Kate went to an English primary school.

Kate Middleton (front row, left) is pictured in a rounders team photo during her time as a pupil at St Andrews School in Pangbourne, Berkshire, England.

The Duchess of Cambridge spent ten years at St Andrews Prep School, in Pangbourne, Berkshire, from age three to thirteen. She enjoyed her time there so much that, when she left aged 13, she told her Mum she wanted to return as a teacher. Kate's sister, Pippa, also attended the prep school. It was while at school that Kate and Pippa, were given their nicknames 'Pip' and 'Squeak'. They even called their pet guinea pigs by the same names. Kate was invited to return in 2012 to open some new sports facilities at the school – and was even seen wielding a hockey stick while wearing heels and a designer coat-dress!

During her two-hour visit, Kate remembered the trees she used to climb, enjoyed her favourite flapjack and rice crispie pudding for lunch and confirmed the high jump record she set when she was a girl - 1.50m - which remains unbeaten today. Headmaster Dr David Livingstone said that as well as the high jump record she set in 1995 she was the leading goal scorer for the hockey team of which she was captain, and still held the joint record for the 4x100 m relay. During her time at St Andrews Prep School, Kate excelled at sport. She has said: "It was while I was here at school that I realised my love of sport. Sport has been a huge part of my life."

Catherine, Duchess of Cambridge takes part in a day of activities and festivities to mark the occasion of
St Andrews Day at St Andrews School on November 30, 2012 in Pangbourne, Berkshire, England.

There are several photos showing her in teams such as hockey and tennis. In fact, contrary to popular ideas that the couple first met at St Andrews University, it was in fact at the prep school that Kate got her first glimpse of Prince William! Aged nine years old at the time, he was due to appear in an away game at the school, playing for his own prep school team, Ludgrove Colts. Apparently there was so much excitement when it was announced that Prince William would be playing in a sports game at the school, that he drew a crowd of admirers on the touchline. Deputy head Paul Outram, who has been at the school for 30 years, said he remembered her as a "cheerful and affable" pupil. As well as being keen on sport, the young Kate Middleton sang in the choir and played the recorder and then the flute in the school orchestra. She also took part in school plays, playing Prince Charming in Cinderella and Eliza Doolittle in My Fair Lady. Kate has said of her time at St Andrews: "I absolutely loved my time here - they were some of my happiest years."

Kate Middleton (front row, centre) is pictured in a hockey team photo during her time as a pupil at St Andrews School in Pangbourne, Berkshire, England.

Bullying

Miss Middleton had been content and popular as a boarder at St Andrews prep school in Pangbourne until she was 13, when she moved to Downe House in Cold Ash, Thatcham near her parents' home, in September 1995. Unfortunately, her time at Downe House was so unhappy, that her parents removed her after just two terms at the school, which charges £10,000 a term. Kate was in a minority at the school, since she was a day student and not a boarder – 90% of the school were boarders at the time. Kate would return to the family home in Bucklebury, Berkshire every evening. It is likely that she was excluded from the popular cliques.

There are reports that some of the girls at Downe House called her names, made life difficult for her by stealing her books and rounded up on her. When Kate would try to sit down with them at lunchtime, they would all get up and sit on another table. Susan Cameron, former Downe House mistress, has admitted that there were problems with teasing and that Kate was unsettled and unhappy, showing her unhappiness by being quiet.

Kate Middleton aged five.

Kate Middleton (back row, 3rd left) is pictured in a tennis team photo during her time as a pupil at St Andrews School in Pangbourne, Berkshire, England.

One source, a former schoolmate at the school, has said: 'In our peer group she was regarded as a nonentity. All the social-climbing girls – and there were lots of them at Downe House – thought she was not worth bothering with.' Allegedly, there was a perception that Kate was 'skinny' and 'meek'. Prince William and the Duchess of Cambridge have since included an anti-bullying charity, Beatbullying, in their new charitable foundation. It's most probably because of Kate's unhappy experience at Downe House.

Marlborough College, Wiltshire. UK.

Marlborough College

After her unhappy experience at Downe House, Kate moved to Marlborough College. Set in rolling grounds on the outskirts of a market town in Wiltshire, the 169 year old boarding school is a remnant of a past age, with red-brick classrooms and a church for Sunday services. Marlborough College was founded in 1843 for the sons of Church of England clergymen and within a few decades it had become one of the country's leading boys' public schools. The school offers education to boarding and non-boarding pupils. Notable alumni include the poet Sir John Betjeman, Princess Eugenie, Samantha Cameron and singer Chris de Burgh. Wearing her new uniform, a blue blazer and tartan skirt, a teenage Kate arrived at the boarding school in April 1996 – midway through the academic year and at the start of the summer term.

Kate soon gained a reputation for being ordinary, hard-working, sporty and easy-going. She was captain of the hockey team and took part in tennis, netball and athletics. Kate was nicknamed 'Princess in Waiting' as a joke. She gained 11 GCSEs at Marlborough College and stayed on to do her 'A' levels, studying Chemistry, Biology and Art. She also completed her Duke of Edinburgh Gold Award whilst at the school. After leaving Marlborough College in July 2000, the Duchess of Cambridge took a gap year. Kate studied at the British Institute in Florence, went on a Raleigh International Programme in Chile and crewed on Round the World Challenge boats in the Solent.

Pippa Middleton, James Middleton, Carole Middleton and Michael Middleton.

The Middletons

Carole Middleton

Carole Middleton was born on 31st January 1955 in Ealing, London. Her full name is Carole Elizabeth Goldsmith – she shares her middle name 'Elizabeth' with her daughter Kate. Carole's father's family came from London. Carole's Dad, Ronald Goldsmith, was a builder. She was raised in a council flat in Southall and went to a local state school. Her maternal line, the Harrisons, were working-class labourers and miners from Sunderland and Country Durham. Carole worked as an airline stewardess for British Airways, which is where she met her husband and Kate's Dad, Michael Middleton.

Carole Middleton attends day three of Royal Ascot, Ladies Day, at Ascot Racecourse on June 21, 2012.

Carole Middleton attends Derby Day at the Investec Derby Festival at Epsom racecourse on June 4, 2011 in Epsom, England.

Carole and Michael were married on the 21st July 1980 at the parish church of St James in Dorney, Buckinghamshire. They set up home in a semi-detached Victorian house near Reading in Berkshire. They have three children – Kate is the oldest, with Pippa next in line, followed by James. The year that James was born (1987), Carole started up 'Party Pieces'. The business began by supplying party bags. Carole said she began the business because she was frustrated trying to find novelty items for her own children's birthday parties. By 1995, both Carole and Michael were running the business full time and the family were able to move into a large five-bed house in Bucklebury, Berkshire. The business was so successful, the Middletons are said to have become self-made millionaires through it. As a result of their wealth, Carole was able to send her children to independent public schools. Carole credits hard work and determination for the success of the business and says that even now she'll stay up into the early hours to fulfil an order. In 2011, international designer Karl Lagerfeld said that Carole Middleton was the most beautiful woman in the Middleton family.

Michael Middleton attends Ladies Day of Royal Ascot at Ascot Racecourse on June 21, 2012 in Ascot, England.

Michael Middleton

Michael Francis Middleton was born in 1949 in Leeds. His Dad was a pilot instructor and aviator and his grandfather was a solicitor. All three generations were educated at Clifton College as boarders. Michael met his future wife, Carole, whilst working for British Airways, where he was an officer. In 1979 Michael was promoted and became a flight dispatcher at London Heathrow airport. His job was to keep track of the airline's fleet on the ground. After Carole set up 'Party Pieces', a business selling party items, Michael joined her and the two ran the highly successful company from 1995. Just before Kate and William got married, Michael was granted his own family coat of arms in April 2011, by the College of Arms.

The senior officer of the College of Arms helped the family with the design. It features three acorn sprigs – these represent each of his children. There is also an oak – which stands for 'England and strength', as well as the family's home of West Berkshire. The dividing line (between colours) echoes the family name, 'Middleton'. There are three white chevrons, symbolising peaks and mountains and they are there to show the family's love of the English Lake District and of skiing. In his speech as father of the bride, Michael referred to a famous incident, where William borrowed a helicopter to go and visit Kate at the family home. 'I knew things were getting serious, when I found a helicopter in my garden. I thought, gosh, he must like my daughter!' joked Michael. Prince William and Michael Middleton are reported to have a close relationship.

*Michael Middleton and Carole Middleton, following the wedding
ceremony of Prince William and their daughter, Kate.*

Party planner Pippa Middleton promotes the Dutch edition of her book 'Celebrate: A Year of British Festivities for Families and Friends' in a bookstore in Harlem.

Pippa Middleton

Pippa Middleton was born Philippa Charlotte Middleton on the 6th September 1983. Just eighteen months after her big sister, Kate. She appeared as maid of honour at Kate and William's wedding, famously in a figure-hugging dress that gained much media attention. The dress was designed by Sarah Burton from the Alexander McQueen fashion house. It was made of ivory crepe with a cowl at the front and organza-covered buttons all the way down the back.

It soon had lots of imitations in high street chains. Pippa and Kate both attended St Andrews School in Pangbourne and both went to the same brownie pack at St Andrews. Pippa followed her older sister to prestigious Marlborough College on a sports/all-rounder scholarship. Her prowess on the hockey pitch was well known, with reports that students would flock to the college's astro-pitch to see her play.

Pippa Middleton, sporting her figure-hugging Maid of Honour dress, designed by Sarah Burton.

She attended university in Edinburgh, where she studied for an English Literature degree. Whilst in Edinburgh, she shared a house with Lord Edward Innes-Ker, a son of the Duke of Roxburghe and Earl Percy, heir apparent to the Dukedom of Northumberland.

After graduation, Pippa worked in PR, promoting luxury products. She then took on an events management job with 'Table Talk', a company that organises corporate events and parties. In 2008, Tatler magazine named Pippa the 'number one society singleton', ahead of Princess Eugenie, Prince William's cousin and son of Fergie and his uncle, Prince Andrew. By April 2012, Time magazine was listing Pippa in its 'top 100 influential people in the world.' She is often credited for her fashion sense. Pippa has dated a string of eligible men.

James Middleton, moments after crossing the finish line of the 88th
Vasaloppet cross country ski marathon in Mora on March 4, 2012.

James Middleton

James William Middleton is the youngest of the three Middleton children and was born on 15th April, 1987. Like his sisters, he went to St Andrews in Pangbourne and from there to top public school, Marlborough College. He followed second sister, Pippa, to the University of Edinburgh, where he studied Environmental Resources Management. However, he chose to leave after just a year to set up his own cake-making business, the Cake Kit Company.

The Cake Kit Company has won several awards since it was launched in 2007. Perhaps James has inherited his entrepreneurial streak from his parents! James says that his family have been a great source of strength and support, as well as advice to him. Although he's added, 'like any other family, we have our moments living and working together.' Friends say James would like to be the next Richard Branson, well-known founder of the Virgin Group and a self-made billionaire. Just before Kate and William's wedding, James set up the Nice Group to oversee all future business developments. James' cake designs have included the traditional and the occasionally risqué!

At Kate and William's wedding, James performed a reading. James is dyslexic and so chose to memorise the reading, rather than mess it up in front of the glittering Westminster Abbey guests and two billion audience, who were watching the wedding around the world. He has also said that he wanted to do his sister and her new husband proud, whether he was reading in Westminster Abbey or a little village church around the corner. James was diagnosed with dyslexia when he was 11.

James Middleton on October 18, 2012 in London, England.

Family Business and Wealth

In 2011 it was estimated that Michael and Carole Middleton could be worth in the region of £30 million. That was before Kate and William got married. Analysts in the City of London decided this was a fair figure to put on the 'Party Pieces' business which the Middletons founded and run together. In Kate's last year at Marlborough college, before she went to St Andrews, where she would meet her princely future husband, the mail-order firm was on the internet, employing ten people and was taking in the region of a thousand orders per week. Now Party Pieces employs at least 30 staff and is based in two converted farmhouses near the family's home in Berkshire.

Kate's brother currently has three businesses registered at Companies House. They are Nice Cakes Ltd, Nice Wine Ltd and Nice Group London Ltd. Like Party Pieces, they're based at the business barns the family uses in Berkshire. The Middleton family contributed to the cost of Kate and Will's wedding, paying out £97,000 for things that included Kate's dress, Pippa's dress, hotel rooms and the royal couple's honeymoon. The couple had also bought Kate a mortgage-free flat in Chelsea.

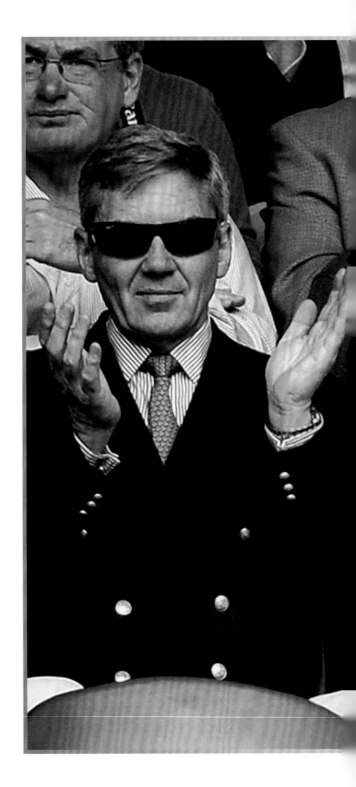

Michael, Carole and Pippa Middleton attend the Wimbledon Tennis Championships at the All England Tennis Club, in southwest London on June 29, 2011.

Carole, James, Michael and Pippa Middleton depart the Goring Hotel in London on April 30, 2011 in London, England.

Family Life

The warmth of normal, family life is possibly one of the reasons Prince William has bonded so closely with the Middleton family. His own mother, Princess Diana, was one of the most photographed women in the world, beautiful and married to the heir of the British throne. But behind closed doors, there was a lot of trouble with Prince Charles and Princess Diana splitting acrimoniously, when William and Harry were only little. Added to that was the tragedy of Diana's untimely death in a road accident in Paris in 1997. William was just a teenager, aged 15, when his mother died and Prince Harry was just 12. Poignantly, the two had to walk behind their mother's funeral procession as it made its way to Westminster Abbey. It's possible that Michael and Carole Middleton, with their happy, settled, and prosperous family life represented what had been missing from William's upbringing.

Michael and Carole Middleton make a statement on the engagement of their daughter Catherine Middleton to Prince William outside their home on November 16, 2010 near the Berkshire village of Bucklebury, England.

With the first baby now here, it's likely that there will be extended family gatherings at Michael and Carole's £4.5 million manor house in Berkshire, where there's plenty of room for family and grandchildren to roam around. The love and stability of family life, which was so important to William's mother Diana, looks likely to continue through William and Kate and in particular through the influence of the Middletons on the Royal family.

Kate Middleton, during her graduation ceremony
at St Andrews, Scotland, 23 June 2005.

University Life

Gap Year

If Kate becomes Queen, she won't just be the first queen to have gone to University, she'll also be the first to have had a gap year. She chose to volunteer on a trip with Operation Raleigh, a long-established provider of trips to developing countries for students and young people. Kate worked on environmental projects and a community programme with underprivileged children in Chile. Strangely enough, William had also been out to Chile with Operation Raleigh, mixing with a diverse range of people. It was even said he was the only person one particularly troubled young man would talk to and William was toasted as the born-storyteller of the group, often recounting stories that had his listeners in hysterics. But it wasn't only working in impoverished conditions that formed Kate's gap year. She also took time out at the British Institute in Florence, a hotbed of Renaissance art treasures.

As part of her cross-cultural experience, Kate would have seen priceless, world-renowned art, such as original Canalettos and Rembrandts, up close and personal, as well as received tuition in Italian for three hours a day and lectures in the Renaissance in the local palazzos, such as the Palazzo dello Strozzino, a palace built in 1458 and the Palazzo Lanfredini, on the south bank of the River Arno. In fact, Kate's future father-in-law, Charles, visited the Institute in 1985 with his then-wife Diana and became one of its patrons.

Diana, Princess of Wales and Prince Charles visit a church on April 23, 1985 in Florence, Italy during the Royal Tour of Italy.

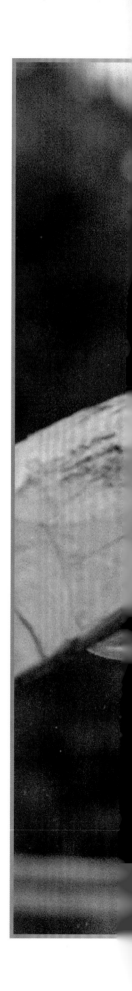

Prince William carries a log used to construct walkways linking buildings during his Raleigh International expedition on December 11, 2000 in Tortel, Chile.

A view of the Andes from Tortel Village, where Prince William stayed during his Raleigh International Expedition in Southern Chile.

Kate Middleton and Prince William on the day of their graduation ceremony at
St Andrews University in St Andrews on June 23, 2005 in Scotland.

What Kate Studied

K ate studied History of Art at St Andrews University – the same course that Prince William began, before switching to Geography in his second year. In fact, in their first academic year, if William missed a class, Kate would take notes for him and they would catch up at the end of the day in their halls of residence. She graduated with a 2:1 in 2005, the same year the Prince graduated. Having a place in St Salvator's hall of residence was likely to have been inspiring for Kate, since it contains big oil paintings by some of the philosophers from the Scottish Enlightenment and has beautiful stained glass windows.

All of her education in art history is likely to be useful to Kate, since the Royal Family's private art collection boasts 7,000 paintings, 500,000 prints and 30,000 drawings and watercolours by some of the world's greatest artists.

New graduate Kate Middleton, wears a traditional gown to the graduation ceremony at St Andrews University to collect her degree in St Andrews on 23rd June, 2005, Scotland.

Kate Middleton on the day of her graduation ceremony at St Andrews University in St Andrews on 23rd June, 2005 in Scotland.

University Life

St Andrews university is, serendipitously, the place where Prince William and Kate Middleton decided to study for their degrees. Had neither of them gone to St Andrews, the modern day fairytale that is the story of their romance would never have happened. But what was university life like for Kate? Having gained three 'A' levels at traditional public school, Marlborough College, Kate opted for another traditional educational establishment – St Andrews University in Scotland. Kate, like many university students, was allocated a hall of residence in which to live during her first year.

Like thousands of previous 'freshers' as first year undergraduates are known, she must have been nervous leaving home and Berkshire for the east of Scotland. But she needn't have worried. The eighteen year old had been given a place in ivy-clad St Salvator's hall, affectionately known as 'Sallies', which was home to almost 200 undergraduates. Another 'fresher' that year was Prince William – and he too had a

place at 'Sallies'. It was here that the pair first met in 2001. Friendship turned to romance when William caught sight of nineteen-year-old Kate strutting her stuff on the catwalk of a charity fashion show the following year. As the two became a couple, it's likely they enjoyed the quiet night-life of St Andrews doing the things that students do – drinking beer and eating curries. In fact there's a framed photo of the young prince at the Jahangir Indian restaurant. Kate and William shared a house in their second and third years of university. Kate encouraged her boyfriend as he pursued his love of rugby and surfing at St Andrews. The pair spent four years studying at St Andrews, as Scottish universities have four year degree courses, unlike English universities, which opt for just three years.

Kate Middleton, arrives for her graduation ceremony at St Andrews, Scotland, 23rd June 2005.

Prince William and Catherine Middleton visit the University of St Andrews, Fife, as patrons of the 600th Anniversary Appeal.

St Andrews

S t Andrews is Scotland's oldest university and dates back as far as 1411. It's set in the picturesque town of St Andrews itself, which is in Fife. The town is full of old cobbled streets and views of the sea. It's home to just 16,000 permanent residents. This combination of tradition and breath-taking beauty may be one of the reasons Kate chose it for her university education. St Andrews is situated 60 miles north of Edinburgh. It's named after St Andrew the apostle, one of the first followers of Jesus, who is credited with bringing Christianity to Scotland. In essence a quaint village, it's famous for two things – the university and its international golf course.

In fact, St Andrews is known as the 'home of golf.' It has links to golf that go back six centuries and has 11 golf courses, one of which is the oldest in the world and is called, fittingly, the Old Course. Locals, students and visitors enjoy the outdoor lifestyle, with walks on the pier and even a spot of surfing. In 2012 the University celebrated its 600th anniversary. The Royal couple attended the event, where William praised St Andrews, for giving him the chance to lead as normal university life as possible. Of course, the Royal Family have had long connections and affection for Scotland. The Queen is a patron of the Highland Games. The Royal Family frequently spend time at Balmoral, the 50,000 acre estate bought by Queen Victoria. Kate and William also have a Scottish title – the Earl and Countess of Strathearn.

St Salvator's Hall, aka Sallies, where Prince William and Kate Middleton lived while attending university.

Prince William, Duke of Cambridge and Catherine, Duchess of Cambridge visits the
UNICEF Centre on November 2, 2011 in Copenhagen, Denmark.

Kate Meets Prince William

Prince William carrying a surfboard as he walks with two friends along the shoreline October, 2004 at St Andrews in Scotland.

Prince William playing pool with friends at a bar on November 15, 2004, in St Andrews University, Scotland.

Friends

Wiliam already had a friend from Eton at St Andrews – Fergus Boyd – and another friend Ollie Chadwyck-Healey. Prince William and his friends became known as 'Sally's boys and included other young students, such as Ali Coutts-Wood, Graham Booth, Charlie Nelson and Ollie Baker. As part of his social life, Prince William joined the water polo team, cycled along the coastline paths and would swim with Kate in the mornings. He'd also hang out at the student union, sometimes for a game of pool. Soon enough, Kate and William were seen spending more time with each other, a relationship that was only set to become more meaningful as time passed.

Prince William in St Salvator's Quad on November 15, 2004, at St Andrews University where he was a student.

See-through dress worn by Kate Middleton during the charity fashion show at St Andrews University in 2002.

Designer Charlotte Todd with her creation, the see-through knitted dress worn by Kate Middleton at St Andrews University charity show in 2002.

The Famous Charity Dress

One night in March 2002, was the annual event 'Don't Walk' fashion show, which raised money for charity. The event took place at the five-star St Andrews Bay Hotel and Kate had agreed to be a model. For her dress, she was given a sheer lace and ribbon number that had been put together by Charlotte Todd. Charlotte had made the black and gold slip dress, while studying fashion and textiles at the University of the West of England in 2000. It had taken her a week to knit together the silk fabrics and to add a blue ribbon strip. Fittingly enough, she had called the dress 'the art of seduction.' The dress in total had cost a mere £30 to make.

Two years after the creation of the dress, St Andrews University asked to borrow it for a fundraising fashion show. At the time, William and Kate were just friends and Kate was dating final year student, Rupert Finch. As Kate sashayed down the catwalk, William became smitten.

William had paid £200 for his front-row ticket, which had given him a glimpse of a different side to demure Kate. At a party after the show, William and Kate huddled together in a corner, deep in conversation. Everyone had noticed how smitten William was with Kate.

Hobbies and Sport

Kate's love of sport, which had begun at St Andrews prep school, continued at Marlborough College, and at university, too. At heart, she was a country girl, who enjoyed playing sport and swimming. Like William, she is also a good skier. Most mornings in their first year, Kate and William would meet as friends and swim at the luxury Old Course Hotel pool. Often, Kate would also go running before breakfast. After a few weeks, William, who sat next to the head table in the halls, would invite Kate to join him and his friends. Health-conscious Kate and William would often have muesli and fruit for breakfast. As part of a second-year house share at 13a Hope Street, Kate and William each paid £100 a week for the two-storey top floor apartment. William had the biggest room, which overlooked a private garden and the back of a student union building.

The two other housemates were Fergus Boyd and Olivia Bleasdale. Everyone shared cleaning of the house and, despite the fact it had been refitted to be fully secure, the house-share gave Kate and William the normality the two students wanted. As a house, they would often throw dinner-parties, in time-honoured student style. William and Fergus would go to the local supermarket to buy ingredients for cooking and also wine. By now, William and Kate were romantically involved, but they decided to keep their romance as under the radar as possible, agreeing never to hold hands in public and turning up at and leaving events separately. By the third year, William and Kate had decided to move out of Hope Street. Together they moved into Balgove House in Strathtyrum, a private estate a quarter of a mile out of town. The extra outbuildings provided housing for William's security team, but the pair were able to enjoy the seclusion and privacy they liked, taking long strolls and having picnics together in the two acres of wild grassland behind the high walls and having their friends visit. It was perhaps Kate's first taste of what royal life would be like and what was to follow. But it wasn't all going to be smooth sailing.

Kate Middleton attending a training session with the Sisterhood on the River Thames, for their cross channel challenge.

Kate Middleton Skiing In Klosters, Switzerland.

Top image; Kate watching synchronised swimming at the London Olympic Games.
Above image; Prince William at the Donald Dewar Leisure Centre on April 4, 2013.

Above image; The Duchess of Cambridge posing with
Team GB on Day 14 of the London 2012 Olympic Games.

Prince William and Kate Middleton whilst on a skiing holiday on March 19, 2008 in Klosters, Switzerland.

Kate Middleton as she arrived at her home in
Chelsea, London on January 9, 2007.

The
Break-up and
Make-up

Before the Split

Immediately following graduation, William travelled to New Zealand, where he represented the Queen, commemorating 60 years since the end of the Second World War. He also spent time with the touring British and Irish Lions rugby team. Following that trip, William took Kate to visit his friend Jessica Craig in Kenya. William wanted to show Kate the beauty of Africa and to share a memorable holiday with her. They stayed at the £1,500 per night Il Ngwesi Lodge. During the day, William worked on the conservation and in the evening he and Kate would spend time together.

The couple also spent time seeing the New Year in together at a cottage on the Queen's Sandringham estate in Norfolk. After the celebrations were over, Kate and William headed off for ski-mecca Kloster, the place where he'd first been photographed by the press putting an arm around his new girlfriend. Speculation was rife at this point, despite an upcoming period of military training at the prestigious Sandhurst Academy. Kate apparently organised a farewell party for William at Clarence House. She was mindful of the fact that they weren't going to see each other nearly as often or easily as they had done at university. She also wanted to share her own birthday celebrations with him – she was about to turn 24 – before he went away. William arrived at Sandhurst in January 2006. He'd been accompanied by his father and by his own private secretary, Jamie Lowther-Pinkerton. William signed in and was given the room which would be his home for the next year. Every officer in the British Army must undertake the gruelling 44-week commissioning course. Just like his royal forbears, now it was William's turn.

Chelsy Davy and Kate Middleton watching Prince Harry and Prince William play in a charity polo match at the Beaufort Polo Club on July 29, 2006 in Tetbury, England.

Kate Middleton and her parents attending the Sovereign's Parade at Sandhurst Military Academy on December 15, 2006 in Surrey, England.

The Split

Despite the fairy-tale romance nature of Kate and William's relationship, it hasn't all been plain sailing. In April 2007, the couple, who were widely tipped to get married, split up. The couple had been under increasing pressure, since leaving university a couple of years previously. William had moved to an army camp with the Blues and Royals in Bovington in Dorset and Kate was continuing her life in London, where she was working as an accessories buyer for a fashion chain. The distance and different lifestyles put a strain on their relationship, which otherwise had appeared stable and steady.

It's likely the pair, who had been living together in St Andrews, had been unable to see each other more than once a week.

The media reported that the two had reached an amicable agreement to part, despite the fact that there had been mounting speculation about a forthcoming engagement, with paparazzi in attendance outside Kate's home and police being called in to help the couple leave a London nightclub. At the time, Kate had no formal protection, although William appealed to the press to leave her alone. Despite the split, Kate attended William's 'passing out' parade from Sandhurst Military Academy the following December, the first time she'd been at an event at the same time as the Queen and other senior royals.

Kate Middleton post break-up,
May 17, 2007, London.

Prince William & Kate Middleton attending the first day of the Cheltenham Festival Race Meeting.

Kate Middleton leaving her Chelsea flat on her 25th birthday on January 9, 2007 in London, England.

Kate Middleton on a night out in London, April 20, 2007.

Time Apart

It was clear that William wanted to split up, while Kate was less happy with the idea. The Duchess of Cambridge has since admitted to feeling angry and upset about the split, although she's also subsequently said that the break was a positive experience and that it ultimately helped to strengthen her and William's partnership.

At the time, the Prince told his girlfriend that he needed 'space.' He felt that they were still trying to find out who they were and what direction they should take in life. Plus, he was enjoying a wilder social life with the 'Booze and Royals' as the Blues and Royals were sometimes known, drinking and partying hard on his time off.

Friends were surprised that, rather than going under with the break-up from William, Kate made a clear decision to get on with her life. It was probably this attitude that made William begin to wonder if he'd made the wrong choice. Not only that, but pictures began to appear in the press of beautiful Kate out on the town – looking stylish and attractive in short dresses that showed off her long legs. Perhaps it was Kate's new found independence that attracted William all over again. Or maybe he started to worry that Kate might get over him and find another man? Perhaps he realised he could lose her forever. Things were about to change…

Kate Middleton spotted with friends on a night out in London, on May 11, 2007.

Prince William and Kate Middleton at the Cheltenham Race Festival, 13 March 2007, just before their split.

Prince Harry and Kate Middleton laugh together as they watch the Order of the Garter procession at Windsor Castle on June 16, 2008 in Windsor, England.

The Make-up

Just as suddenly as they split, there were signs that a reconciliation was in the air for Kate and William. By June, just 10 weeks after the break-up, Kate joined William at a Moulin Rouge-themed fancy dress party at Sandhurst in Bovington. The couple apparently kissed on the dance-floor and then made their excuses, leaving for the privacy of William's room. Despite appearances, the couple still said they were 'just good friends.' Yet the following month, Kate went to the Concert For Diana, which was being held at Wembley Stadium and was in honour of William's mum. The night before the gig, she stayed at Clarence House and at the party afterwards, she and William shared a dance. It seemed their love had been rekindled and the pair jetted off to Desroches Island in the Seychelles for a romantic break together.

Prince William and Prince Harry and guests Chelsy Davy and Kate Middleton watch the Concert for Diana at Wembley Stadium on July 1, 2007 in London, England.

Prince William and Kate Middleton whilst on a skiing holiday on March 19, 2008 in Klosters, Switzerland.

After the trip, William returned to Sandhurst, where he passed as an officer in the following December. By April 2008, Kate and William were firmly back together and Kate was on her second official public engagement as his girlfriend, watching him receive his Wings as part of his RAF and Navy training. By September, William knew what he wanted to do – train to become a full-time RAF Search and Rescue pilot. It would mean more time apart for the couple, but Kate knew it would no longer be a problem. It seemed the relationship was secure and trusting. By now, Kate had quit her London job and was instead working for the family firm, 'Party Pieces.' Rumours of engagement were still rife, but instead of a flat out refusal to consider them, it seemed that William and Kate were making their own secret plans to their own timetable. William passed his Search and Rescue training at RAF Valley by September 2009 and during an official tour of New Zealand and Australia at the beginning of 2010, in response to people asking him, 'when are you going to marry Kate?', William replied with a smile, 'wait and see.'

The Duchess of Cambridge arriving at the BAFTA Brits at the
Belasco Theatre on July 9, 2011 in Los Angeles, California.

Style
Icon

Style Icon

Kate's style varies enormously, depending on whether she's at a royal function or hanging out with William and their friends. But whatever she wears, it usually says something about her personality, whether it's demure and designer or practical and sporty. And it's clear her style carries influence – high street stores always reveal an uptake in sales after Kate's been spotted wearing something, whether that's coral jeans and a sweatshirt or 'that dress' in her engagement photos. Jeans, boots, a comfy sweater and a funky leather hat are good enough for an outdoor gig, showing that Kate's a royal who's not about to fall into the trap of fuddy-duddy. She likes the laid-back look for supporting William on the polo field – often it's jeans, flats, a smart top and a leather jacket. But she's not a jeans-only kind of girl. Kate also favours floaty, floral numbers.

She likes to wear dresses in colder weather, too, and her slim figure means she can get away with chunkier knitted dresses and tight, wide belts. When it comes to colour, Kate's not afraid to go for vivid hues, from bright green to emerald blue. And when it comes to a night out on the town, Kate likes her dresses and skirts short, teamed with high heels and a fashionable clutch. Of course, when it comes to official engagements, Kate rarely puts a foot wrong – hats, heels and tight-belted skirts and dresses, perhaps with a well-cut coat – mean the Duchess always looks chic and glamorous. And for those extra special celebrations, a floor-skimming lacy dress is just right. It's no wonder the crowd are often looking at her – and not her husband!

Kate Middleton arriving at the Day-Glo Midnight Roller Disco at
The Renaissance Rooms on September 17, 2008 in London, England.

*Kate Middleton watching Prince William and Prince Harry
compete in The Dorchester Trophy polo match at Cirencester
Park Polo Club on June 7, 2009 in Cirencester, England.*

*The Duchess of Cambridge attending the National
Review of Queen's Scouts at Windsor Castle on
April 21, 2013 in Windsor, England.*

How Her Style Changed

Kate's style over the decade or so that she's known Prince William has changed from conservative 'Home Counties' girl to elegant and chic. In her early days of dating Prince William, she looked like a typical, middle-class student, favouring chunky knits (against the bracing Scottish coastal air) and belted jeans. Even on the couple's first skiing trip together, she looked like every other girl from a slightly privileged background, having fun on the slopes. Of course, there was that moment, when she wore a £30 lacy knit see-through dress at a charity fashion event and caught William's eye. Three years into her relationship with Prince William, she was photographed at the Game Fair in Blenheim Palace, wearing a tweedy-looking ensemble of long coat and short skirt, with a sharp shirt, wide belt and Penelope Chilvers boots.

A year later, she wore a lace pencil skirt, fitted cream blazer and neat black fascinator in her hair to the summer wedding of mutual pals, Hugh Van Cutsem Junior and Rose Astor. William was an usher at the wedding. At another wedding, this time in 2006 between Laura Parker-Bowles and Harry Lopes, Kate wore a knee-length cream fitted coat, with matching headpiece and shoes. She was starting to look very co-ordinated and chic, finding an unfussy, yet classy style that suited her figure. At the end of the year, Kate chose to wear a striking black and red outfit for the Sovereign's Parade at Sandhurst, where William was graduating as officer. It was at this event that the Queen was in attendance – somehow lending credibility to the idea that she approved of her grandson's choice of partner.

Kate Middleton, arriving at the society wedding of Hugh Van Cutsem Junior to Rose Astor at Burford Parish Church on June 4, 2005 in Burford, England.

Kate Middleton, attending the wedding of Laura Parker Bowles and Harry Lopes at St Cyriac's Church, Lacock on May 6, 2006 in Wiltshire, England.

Famous Outfits

To announce the royal engagement in November 2010, Kate wore a sapphire wrap dress by Issa, a colour that matched her new engagement ring - the ring that had famously belonged to William's mother, Diana. The dress sold out immediately in stores after she wore it. A month later Kate was in Belfast, Northern Ireland, wearing a double-breasted khaki trench coat by Burberry. Again, the coat sold out within hours of Kate being photographed wearing it. On her wedding night in April 2011, Kate changed into a satin gown and angora bolero by Sarah Burton for Steve McQueen – the same designer who'd created her wedding dress. Boleros immediately became fashion items for brides that year. By May, Kate was meeting Michelle Obama, another global style icon. Fresh from honeymooning in the Seychelles, a tanned Kate wore a camel-colour cap sleeve dress by Reiss. In June of the same year, Kate made an appearance at the Derby at Epsom Downs, wearing another Reiss number, this time a floaty chiffon dress, with a hat by Whiteley, jacket by Joseph and nude pumps by her favourite footwear people, LK Bennett.

It was a lot more minimal for tennis at Wimbledon – this time Kate wore a sporty little white number by Temperley. She could almost have been on court! On the 1st of July 2011, William and Kate were at Canada Day celebrations. For the evening event, Kate chose a royal purple Issa dress, similar in shape to the one she'd worn for her engagement announcement. She added an Anya Hindmarch clutch. A couple of days later, the Duchess chose a navy Erdem dress for a Freedom of the City Ceremony in Quebec. After that, Kate went on a visit to Prince Edward Island, the setting of one of her favourite stories, Anne of Green Gables. Her knit cream dress by Alexander McQueen could have come out of the same wholesome story! It was more Jenny Packham in Calgary, when Kate sported a bespoke yellow dress by the designer. What was on her feet? LK Bennett of course! For a visit to Calgary zoo, the Duchess wore a red coat dress by Catherine Walker – on the lapel was Queen Elizabeth's maple leaf brooch.

The Duchess of Cambridge attending a welcome ceremony at Province House on day 5 of the Royal Couple's North American Tour, July 4, 2011 in Charlottetown, Prince Edward Island, Canada.

*Prince William and Kate Middleton posing for
photographs following their engagement announcement.*

The Duchess of Cambridge arriving at the Foundation Polo Challenge held at the
Santa Barbara Polo and Racquet Club on July 9, 2011 in Santa Barbara, California.

Arriving at the Foundation Polo Challenge, Kate opted for a silk frock by Jenny Packham, with her favourite nude leather sandals and a straw clutch. Earrings were from Kiki McDonough. By evening, she'd changed again, to attend the BAFTA 'Brits To Watch' event. This time she was wearing a lavender Alexander McQueen dress, sandals and a clutch by Jimmy Choo and a pair of diamond chandelier earrings, on loan from William's grandmother, the Queen.

It was back to high street fashion for an event in California on July 10th 2011, where she wore a top and skirt from Whistles with navy pumps, a clutch and sapphire earrings (blue is said to be the Duchess' favourite colour). The following September Kate supported the opening of a children's unit at the Royal Marsden cancer centre in London wearing a three-quarter sleeve Amanda Wakeley dress. Unsurprisingly the dress sold out almost as soon as the public had seen Kate in it.

There were also glittering parties to attend – in October the royal couple were at a black tie charity dinner, where Kate chose a Beulah London red dress. Red was the colour she chose to visit the UNICEF Global Supply Center in Copenhagen, the following month. This time it was a tailored red wool coat by LK Bennett with Stuart Weitzman suede boots. Kate then chose a chiffon and satin Jenny Packham dress for the November National Memorial Arboretum Appeal reception at St James Palace.

In December at the Prince's Trust concert in the Albert Hall, the Duchess opted for a dress by Zara with a Ralph Lauren jacket. A few days before Christmas Eve, Kate visited the Centrepoint homeless charity in London – wearing a Ralph Lauren turtleneck sweater dress and black Aquatalia boots. For Christmas Day and a traditional service at St Mary Magdalene church, the Duchess wore a dark purple fitted coat, Jane Corbett trilby and black heels.

The Duchess of Cambridge attending a BAFTA reception at the Belasco Theatre, Los Angeles.

The Duchess of Cambridge attending the Christmas Day service at Sandringham, December 25, 2011.

Back to formal duties, Kate wore a green coat-dress by Emilia Wickstead for celebrations at the Irish Guard barracks for St Patrick's Day. By May, the UK was beginning to gear up for the London Olympics and Kate went to an Olympic-themed concert at the Royal Albert Hall. In the warm weather, she chose a teal Jenny Packham dress with a jewelled waistline. Later the same month, the Duke and Duchess of Cambridge attended a luncheon at Windsor Castle to celebrate the Queen's jubilee. Here Kate chose a knee-length pink dress by Emilia Wickstead. A similar knee-high, pleated dress, albeit in red, was Kate's choice to wear on the Queen's public celebration of her Jubilee aboard a boat on the River Thames.

The dress was by Alexander McQueen and she added her favourite nude LK Bennett heels and Kiki McDonough citrine drop earrings, plus a red hat. For the Olympic torch relay outside Buckingham Palace on July 25th, Kate chose blue skinny jeans, a polo shirt and Stuart Weistzman wedges. Two days later the Games officially opened - William and Kate were in attendance. Kate chose a bespoke, satin blue outfit by Christopher Kane. Back at Wimbledon to watch Murray claim his first Olympic title, Kate opted for a blue Stella McCartney dress and Smythe blazer. Meeting Team GB at the beginning of August, Kate wore a skinnies/blazer/wedges combo, but this time the blazer was from high-street chain Zara. By the end of August, it was the turn of the Paralympians - Kate attended the Opening Ceremony wearing an ivory brocade dress by Jane Troughton.

The Duchess of Cambridge ready to board the royal barge 'Spirit of Chartwell' for the Thames Diamond Jubilee Pageant on the River Thames in London, on June 3, 2012 in London, England.

*The Duchess of Cambridge attending a gala
celebration of Team GB And Paralympics GB
at the Royal Albert Hall, London.*

*Catherine, Duchess of Cambridge
at Buckingham Palace watching the
London 2012 Olympic Torch Relay.*

*Catherine, Duchess of Cambridge
attending the UK premiere of War
Horse at Odeon Leicester Square on
January 8, 2012 in London.*

For Remembrance Day, Kate chose a sombre Diane Von Furstenberg black coat onto which she pinned a poppy brooch sold by the Royal British Legion, who support veteran soldiers. Later in November it was off to the rugby to watch Wales v New Zealand in Cardiff. Kate sported a red wool coat and Gucci clutch. There was more sport – but this time for Kate herself – when she visited her old prep school, St Andrews in Pangbourne. Here she wore a navy and green tartan coat and black boots – which didn't stop her from picking up a hockey stick and running around the pitch! That's style! So whether it's on official royal tours, meeting and greeting the public, out for film or theatre premieres, at receptions or dinners, visiting charity projects or simply walking in the park, Kate always proves she has real style.

*The Duchess of Cambridge attending
the Remembrance Day Ceremony at
the Cenotaph on November 13, 2011
in London, United Kingdom.*

The Duke and Duchess of Cambridge standing together during a jubilee lunch hosted by Queen Elizabeth II, at Windsor Castle on May 18, 2012.

Catherine, Duchess of Cambridge arriving at the Autumn International rugby match between Wales and New Zealand at the Millennium Stadium, Cardiff on November 24, 2012.

Hair and Make-Up

Kate has flawless skin, glossy hair and perfect make-up whatever the occasion and whatever the weather. How does she achieve it? Here are some of her make-up and hair secrets. For her skin, Kate chooses Karin Herzog, a brand of skincare products that's infused with oxygen to keep the complexion glowing.

Soon after she and William were engaged, stepmother-in-law Camilla gave Kate a pot of face mask from Deborah Mitchell, which uses bee venom. Kate followed it up with a facial from the lady herself (costing around £165). But how does she keep her long brunette hair looking so immaculate? That's down to the Richard Ward salon, just off the King's Road in London. Kate has been a regular client at the salon for a number of years. A haircut with the director, Richard Ward, costs around £200. It's believed Kate goes for a cut every two or three months – but it's also likely she has a bespoke blow-dry two or three times a week.

When it comes to make-up, Kate likes to do her own thing. She's been spotted in the beauty hall at Peter Jones in Sloane Square and it's even rumoured she did her own wedding make-up. She's also said to like Jo Malone products, including scented candles in orange blossom, grapefruit and lime and basil and mandarin. To give her the ultimate glow, Kate also has a light spray tan – probably from either Xen-Tan or Urban Retreat.

The Duchess of Cambridge sporting a beautiful up-do at the Royal Albert Hall on May 11, 2012 in London, England.

Catherine, Duchess of Cambridge, visiting the 'Expanding Horizons' Primary school camp at Margaret MacMillan house in Wrotham, Kent, on June 17, 2012.

Role Model

Kate is a new role model of the 21st century for many reasons. Perhaps first of all, it's because of her working class roots. Her mother comes from a line of hard-working Northern families, who worked down the coal-pits or as labourers. And Mum, Carole, herself, was an airline stewardess before she met and married her husband, Michael. Added to that, Michael's a staunch family man. When his job moved him out to the Middle East Michael took his whole family with him. Of course, Kate has had her privileges – going to fee-paying schools St Andrews and prestigious Marlborough College – but she's stayed down-to-earth and unspoiled throughout all of it. In fact, it was said she was quite shy and retiring while a teenager at Marlborough College and kept her feet on the ground.

Another reason the Duchess is touted as a good role model is because she always behaves with impeccable politeness and warmth. Whenever she's chatting to crowds or visiting a project or talking to school-children, the Duchess seems genuinely interested in the people she's talking to. It's a gift that William's mother, Diana, had and it

seems his wife has it, too – and it's certainly something that makes her popular with the British public. Added to that, Kate always dresses stylishly, but without being extravagant.

Far from taking advantage of her own family's wealth or the inherited wealth of her husband, Kate prefers to stick to the tried and trusted when it comes to her looks and dress sense. She's not afraid to recycle a look or wear a dress to a public outing more than once, either. The couple have also set up a foundation which supports charities and social work that is meaningful to both of them, including anti-bullying and conservation projects. Some of Kate's down-to-earth warmth may come from her close family ties – another reason she's a popular role model. Many feel that she'll make an excellent mother. And, what's more, it's clear that William and Kate, whatever the stumbling blocks they've overcome on the way, are in love with each other and want the best for each other and those around them. Those are role model values that never change.

Catherine, Duchess of Cambridge, sitting in a makeshift tent with children as she visited the 'Expanding Horizons' Primary school camp.

Prince William and Kate Middleton, St James' Palace, London.

The Engagement

*Prince William and Kate Middleton officially announce their engagement
at St James's Palace on November 16, 2010 in London, England.*

The Proposal

It was in Africa that Prince William decided to propose to Kate. The couple were enjoying a stop-over in the Rutundu Log Cabins during their Kenyan holiday, when Prince William asked Kate to marry him. Rutundu Log Cabins are very basic – just two small lodges in the style of Alaskan log cabins - far off the beaten track, but an ultimate romantic getaway. They are on the northern slopes of Mount Kenya, Africa's second highest mountain, in an area of wilderness and outstanding natural beauty. As well as simply relaxing, there are opportunities to hike in the fresh air and to spot local game, such as buffalo, leopard and zebra in the tundra around the cabins. There are open fires to keep the chill off at night and moss is stuffed between the cracks of the logs that the lodges are built from to keep them cosy. The couple would have spent their first night together in a small four-poster bed carved from local wood and covered with a simple quilt. Apparently the then 28 year old prince got down on one knee on the verandah of the cabin and presented Kate with the diamond and sapphire engagement ring, which had famously belonged to his late mother, Diana. William later confessed he'd been carrying the almost priceless ring around in his rucksack for the entire trip, looking for the right moment to propose. William has also said that giving this precious ring to Kate was his way of them involving his mother in their wedding and also an expression of how special Kate is to him. How romantic!

Prince William and Kate Middleton pose for photographs in the State Apartments
of St James Palace on November 16, 2010 in London, England.

Lake Rutundu Lodge, Mount Kenya.

After Kate had said yes, they toasted their new status as an engaged couple with a bottle of Champagne, which had been kept cool in a wooden cupboard, before having a meal together, which was prepared by the staff at the African lodgings. Kate and William are then said to have snuggled happily together in front of the fire. Prince William had first visited the lodge two years previously – it's only accessible if you're prepared to hike 15km from the nearest road or get there by air or horseback. Of course, Kenya is also where William's grandmother was told that she was going to become Queen – then Princess Elizabeth was staying at the Treetop Lodge in Nyeri with husband Prince Philip. Asked back home how she felt about William's proposal, Kate said it was 'very romantic.' William revealed that he'd told the Queen and other members of the Royal Family, including brother Harry, to whom he said 'you've got a sister.' William had also asked permission from Kate's Dad, Michael Middleton. The engagement was officially announced on social media, including Facebook and Twitter. When William was asked why he'd decided to propose after eight years of dating, he said simply that it was the right time to do it and that he and Kate were very happy. All that remained was to set the date.

Prince William and Kate Middleton officially announce their engagement at St James's Palace on November 16, 2010 in London, England.

The Ring

When Prince William popped the question to Kate, he used the ring that had belonged to his mother, Diana. The ring is an oval blue 18-carat sapphire and diamond ring. William said of the ring, 'It is very special to me. It was my way to make sure my mother did not miss out on today and the excitement that we are going to spend the rest of our lives together. William's mother Diana tragically died in Paris in 1997. She chose the cluster ring after becoming engaged to Prince Charles in 1981. At that time it cost £28,000 and was part of a selection that was offered to Diana by jewellers Garrard, in February 1981. George Wickes founded Garrard in London in 1735 and it is headquartered in Mayfair with a store also in New York. Garrard has had a long association with the royal family, as Wickes gained the patronage of Frederick, Prince of Wales. In 1843, Queen Victoria appointed Garrard to the position of Crown Jeweller.

Garrard is also responsible for the upkeep of the Crown Jewels and has created memorable royal jewellery pieces, such as the Imperial Crown of India in 1911 and the crown of Queen Elizabeth in 1937. Diana's ring, unusually, was not a bespoke ring and anyone could have bought it before Prince Charles bought it for his first wife. In today's prices the sapphire ring surrounded by 14 diamonds, would cost nearer the £85,000 mark – although with its sentimental value, it's beyond price. The ring became one of the most famous pieces of jewellery in the world. Following Diana's death in 1997, the ring was given to William and placed in a safe. Only William and Harry had access to it.

A close up of Kate Middleton's engagement ring.

Diana, Princess of Wales is photographed wearing her engagement ring at a dinner held by President Ghulam Ishaq Khan in Islamabad during her official visit to Pakistan, September 1991.

*Lady Diana Spencer revealing her sapphire and diamond engagement
ring, while she and Prince Charles pose for photographs in the grounds of
Buckingham Palace, following the announcement of their engagement.*

Prince William and Kate Middleton pose for photographs in the State Apartments of St James Palace on November 16, 2010 in London, England, following the announcement of their engagement.

Interviews and Pictures

As well as sharing the news with family and friends, Kate and William had a duty to share it with the nation - and the world. That's why they set up a TV interview with Tom Bradby of ITV news. Bradby had established a rapport and trust with Prince William over a number of years, so when Buckingham Palace called him to tell him the good news and to ask him to conduct an interview, Bradby wasn't completely surprised. The interview itself took place in one of the rooms at Buckingham Palace, that had already been cleared for an evening function. Bradby began by asking William where, how and when he'd proposed to Kate. According to friends and those who know him well, Prince William has a good, dry sense of humour. He told Bradby that he'd proposed while on holiday in Kenya and had 'taken Kate somewhere nice and proposed to her.' Kate laughed at William's words and affirmed that in fact he had been very romantic. It turned out that Kate hadn't been expecting the proposal at all and she confessed that it was a 'total shock', although she was also 'very excited.'

Kate Middleton posing for photographs
following engagement to Prince William.

Prince William and fiancée Kate Middleton arriving for a Christmas reception in aid of the Teenager Cancer Trust on December 18, 2010 in Fakenham, England.

The two also talked about Kate's engagement ring, which Kate described as 'beautiful' and 'very, very special.' Although the pair were excited and happy, William said he also felt quite nervous – 'we're like ducks, very calm on the surface with little feet going under the water. It's been really exciting because we've been talking about it for a long time, so, for us, it's a real relief and it's really nice to be able to tell everybody.' William also joked that he'd asked Kate's Dad, Michael, after he'd asked Kate, just in case Michael Middleton had refused him permission to marry his daughter! Kate said that her mother was 'absolutely over the moon', Kate acknowledged how important her close-knit family was to her and how they'd helped her through some difficult times.

Questioned about starting a family, Kate alluded to hopes that she
and William would have a happy family together and William agreed.
William spoke about meeting Kate and how they were friends for over
a year before they got romantically involved. He said that things just
'blossomed' from then on. 'We just spent more time with each other
and had a good giggle, had lots of fun and realised we shared the same
interests and had a really good time.' William said of his then-future
wife that Kate has a 'really naughty' sense of humour, which matched
his dry sense of humour. Kate on the other hand recalled being very
shy about meeting Prince William and said she 'scuttled off' after their
first meeting, but agreed that the two became close friends from quite
early on in their time at St Andrews. When asked about the rumour
that she had a picture of Prince William on her wall as a teenager,
William interrupted and claimed it wasn't just one – it was 20! Kate
quickly replied, 'he wishes', before setting the record straight and
saying it was a picture of the Levis guy (an iconic poster).

Prince William and Kate Middleton pose for photographs
following their televised interview with Tom Bradby of ITV News.

The front pages of British national newspapers following the announcement of the royal engagement of Prince William and Kate Middleton.

Asked about what it was like to meet the royal family and William's father, Prince Charles, Kate admitted to being very nervous, but she said, Prince Charles was 'very, very welcoming, very friendly.' She said that the Queen had also been very welcoming. When asked about the time the couple briefly split up, Kate merely said that when you go out for a long time, you get to know each other very well and you go through both good and bad times. If you can come out of the bad times stronger and learn things about yourself, it can be a good thing overall. Finally, the interview ended with allusions to Diana, Prince William's mother, whose engagement ring Kate was wearing. Kate referred to Diana and other members of the royal family as 'inspirational', but

William kept his focus on Kate, ending by saying, 'It's about making your own future and your own destiny and Kate will do a very good job of that.' Ahh! The interview was broadcast around the world the same day. As well as interviews, world-famous photographer Mario Testino, who also photographed Diana for Vanity Fair in 1997, took official engagement photos. The photographs were taken on November 25th, nine days after the couple made their engagement announcement. In the photos, William wraps his bride-to-be in a tender, protective embrace, heads close together, with Kate's hand on William's chest - both of them are smiling radiantly, as befits a couple in love.

Members of the media congregate opposite Buckingham Palace, after
the announcement of the engagement of Britain's Prince William and his
girlfriend Kate Middleton, in central London on November 16, 2010.

Parents of Kate Middleton, Michael and Carole Middleton, make a statement following the engagement of their daughter to Prince William, outside their home near the village of Bucklebury on November 16, 2010 in Berkshire, United Kingdom.

Catherine Middleton gives the crowd one last wave as she enters
Westminster Abbey on April 29, 2011 in London, England.

The Wedding

Wedding Preparations

On the 16th November 2010, Clarence House announced that Prince William was to marry Catherine Middleton 'in the spring or summer of 2011 in London.' The Queen gave her consent on the morning of the engagement, in line with the Royal Marriages Act 1772. As soon as the official engagement was announced, preparations began for the royal wedding. Like any wedding it was bound to be a stressful time, with decisions such as where and when to have the wedding, who to invite, what kind of dress to have, how many bridesmaids, who would be the best-man or maid of honour, what kind of service to have, where to go on honeymoon, where to live after the wedding, which hymns and readings to choose, where to hold the reception, what about booking entertainment and food – let alone how to cope with the in-laws! Factor in a royal wedding, in London, watched by millions of people around the world, and the wedding preparations suddenly took on a whole new meaning. So what did Kate and William do to prepare for their big day? First, Kate and William had to decide when to get married. They opted for a wedding date of Friday, the 29th April 2011.

Next, they had to decide where. They chose Westminster Abbey in London. They chose the Dean of Westminster, John Hall, to preside at the wedding and asked the Archbishop of Canterbury, as befits his role, to conduct the wedding service itself. At the time, that was Rowan Williams. The Bishop of London, Richard Chartres, gave the sermon and Kate's brother, James, gave the reading. By January it had been decided that the ceremony would be at 11am and that the bride would arrive by car, not carriage. The route was to go along The Mall, through Horse Guards Parade, down Whitehall and to Westminster Abbey. For his best man, Prince William asked his brother, Harry and for her maid of honour, Kate asked her sister, Pippa. As well as close family and friends, invitations were sent out to heads of state, foreign royals, diplomats, politicians and celebrities. Since the wedding was not a full state occasion, Kate and William were able to choose many of the eventual 1,900 attendees themselves! The day itself was declared a national holiday, not only in the UK, but throughout the commonwealth, in countries such as Bermuda, the Cayman Islands, Gibraltar, Guernsey, Jersey and the Isle of Man. There were many ceremonial aspects, including the use of state carriages and involving Foot Guards and the Household Cavalry. Before the wedding, the Queen conferred on Prince William the titles: Duke of Cambridge and Earl of Strathearn and Baron Carrickfergus. Kate therefore became Her Royal Highness, the Duchess of Cambridge.

William and Kate decided that they would continue to live in Anglesey after the wedding, where William was based as an RAF Search & Rescue pilot. Instead of wedding gifts, the couple set up the Prince William and Miss Catherine Middleton Charitable Gift Fund, to which well-wishers could donate for charity.

Newlyweds, Kate and William kiss on the balcony at Buckingham Palace on April 29, 2011 in London, England.

Kate Middleton, arriving at the Goring Hotel where she spent her last night as a unmarried woman ahead of the Royal Wedding on April 28, 2011 in London, England.

Kate Middleton arriving at Westminster Abbey for her wedding.

*Kate Middleton with her father Michael Middleton,
at Westminster Abbey on April 29, 2011*

*The Duchess of Cambridge following her
marriage to Prince William.*

Kate's Wedding Dress

I t was the dress everyone was going to be looking at in 2011 –
the wedding dress of Kate Middleton, bride to Prince William.
Kept under wraps, like every bride's outfit, the dress was a well
kept secret up until the big day. But Kate had been heavily involved
in the dress design, choosing Sarah Burton from UK fashion house,
Alexander McQueen, to make it for her. It was an intricate dress of
style and simplicity. Individual flowers were cut from lace and applied
to ivory silk tulle to create a unique design of roses, thistles, daffodils
and shamrocks representing England, Scotland, Ireland and Wales.

Matching shoes were also hand-made from ivory duchesse satin
with lace embroidery. The classic style of Kate's dress may have
been inspired by the wedding outfit of Grace Kelly, who became
Princess Grace of Monaco, when she married Ranier III, Prince of
Monaco in 1956. Like Kate, Grace Kelly was a beautiful woman, yet
a commoner, who married into royalty. Both Grace and Kate's dresses
have high waists, full skirts and a long train. Both were worn with
a sheer veil and diamond tiara. In fact, the tiara was the 'something
borrowed' for Kate's outfit and had been loaned for the day by the
Queen. It was a 1936 Halo tiara by Cartier. Kate opted to wear her
hair loose, in a demi-chignon. Fashion critics around the world hailed
the dress a success. But what did hubby-to-be, Prince William think?
He was the last to see the dress, after all. Apparently, as Kate arrived
by his side in the Abbey, he leaned across and whispered, in romantic
groom fashion, 'you look beautiful.' Just what every bride wants to
hear on her big day!

Pippa's Dress and Kate's Make-Up

As maid of honour, Pippa Middleton could expect to be overshadowed on her big sister's big day, but not in that dress! To approval everywhere, Pippa dressed in another Alexander McQueen creation and, as she bent to adjust her sister's wedding train outside the great doors of Westminster Abbey and then to carry it in, everyone noticed just how good she looked in it. Pippa later said it was weekly pilates which had helped to shape and tone her to look good on the day. Pippa wore a slinky, cream long dress made of ivory satin crepe, with the same embroidery and buttons as Kate's dress. Pippa's dress, however, varied with capped sleeves and a low-slung cowl neckline, which showed off Pippa's dark, but tasteful tan.

The dress should have given confidence to Pippa, who had some big responsibilities on the day, including walking down the aisle hand-in-hand with the youngest two bridesmaids, Grace van Cutsem and Eliza Lopes, both aged just three. Pippa was followed by Margarita Armstrong-Jones (aged eight), Louise Windsor (aged seven), Billy Lowther-Pinkterton (aged ten) and Tom Pettifer (aged eight). Pippa also chose to wear her hair half-up and half-down with a clip of lily-of-the-valley flowers at the back. Michael and Carole had given their second daughter a pair of floral diamond earrings to mark the big day, which she wore as a final touch to her outfit. Both sisters had received guidance from their favourite cosmetics brand, Bobbi Brown, on make-up for the day. It's rumoured Kate even did her own. Now there are two confident sisters!

Kate Middleton arriving with her sister, Pippa Middleton, at the west door of Westminster Abbey.

The Duke and Duchess of Cambridge exit Westminster Abbey after their royal wedding.

Kate Middleton arriving with her sister, Pippa Middleton, at the west door of Westminster Abbey.

The Duke and Duchess of Cambridge exit Westminster Abbey after their royal wedding.

Wedding Party

There were four bridesmaids and two pageboys. Prince William wore the uniform of the Blues and Royals with aiguilettes, a cross-belt and gold waist belt with sword slings, but no sword! Prince Harry wore the wing of the Army Air Corps and the Golden Jubilee and Afghanistan Campaign medals.

The first bridesmaid was Lady Louise Windsor, the seven year old daughter of William's uncle, Prince Edward and his wife, the Countess of Wessex. There was also Margarita Armstrong-Jones, the eight year old daughter of the Viscount and Viscountess Linley. Grace van Custem, the three year old daughter of Kate and William's friend, Hugh van Custem was also a bridesmaid. As was Eliza Lopes the three year old granddaughter of the Duchess of Cornwall. Of the two page-boys, one was William Lowther-Pinkerton, the ten year old son of William's private secretary, Major Jamie Lowther-Pinkerton. And the other was Tom Pettifer, the eight year old son of Prince William and Prince Harry's former nanny, 'Tiggy' Pettifer. For their dresses, the four bridesmaids wore dresses designed by Nicki Macfarlane. She'd made the dresses with the help of her own daughter, Charlotte, at home.

Prince Harry and Prince William arrive at Westminster Abbey prior to his wedding with Kate Middleton in central London on April 29, 2011.

They had full skirts, 'like ballerinas' and were hand-finished with English Cluny lace. Inspired by her Mum's own wedding look, Kate chose ivy and lily-of-the-valley hair wreaths for her little bridesmaids, who looked very cute on the day. The girls also wore satin pumps with a Swarovski crystal buckle. The boys' outfits were designed by Kashket and Partners and were to have the style of 'a foot guard officer at the time of the Regency', with an insignia from the Irish Guards, whose colonel is Prince William. Their look was completed with a smart gold and crimson sash.

Prince William and his wife Kate, followed by best man Prince Harry and maid of honour Pippa Middleton leave Westminster Abbey after their wedding service.

The Venue

The venue for Kate and William's wedding was Westminster Abbey. Westminster Abbey was founded in 960 AD. Kings and Queens have been big benefactors of the Abbey, giving lands, money and even buildings to it. When Henry III was buried at Westminster Abbey in 1272, it established Westminster as the principal royal burial place for the next half a millennium. The Abbey is the traditional venue for royal events, like coronations, although it wasn't used for royal weddings until the 1900s. Princess Patricia, a granddaughter of Queen Victoria, began the trend.

Before then, most royal weddings took place in royal chapels, such as the Chapel Royal of St James' Palace and St George's Chapel, Windsor Castle. Royal weddings held at the Abbey include those of Princess Elizabeth (later Queen Elizabeth II) to the Duke of Edinburgh in 1947, Princess Margaret to Antony Armstrong-Jones (later the Earl of Snowdon) in 1960, Princess Anne (later the Princess Royal) to Mark Phillips in 1973 and the Duke of York to Sarah Ferguson in 1986.

Interestingly, the wedding of William's parents, Prince Charles and Lady Diana Spencer did not take place at Westminster Abbey, but at St Paul's Cathedral in London. Westminster Abbey was, however, where the funeral of Diana had taken place – an event which William attended as a teenager. Diana's body had been laid in the chapel of St James' Palace, before the funeral. Kate and William chose to line the inside of the Abbey with an avenue of 20-foot tall trees – six field maple and two hornbeams – arranged either side of the main aisle, lending the interior an airy, fresh feel. The Abbey has a seating capacity of around 2,000.

A general view of Westminster Abbey during the royal wedding.

*Guests stand for the arrival
of Queen Elizabeth II.*

Guest List

O n the 16th and 17th of February, 2011 three sets of guest lists were sent out in the name of the Queen. The first list was invitations to the wedding itself in Westminster Abbey and consisted of about 1,900 people. The second list was invitations to the luncheon reception at Buckingham Palace, which went out to about 600 people. And the third list, of about 300 names, was for an evening dinner hosted by the Prince of Wales. Over half the people who came to Kate and William's wedding were friends and family.

David and Victoria Beckham arrive to attend the royal wedding.

Prince Edward, the Countess of Wessex, the Duchess of Kent, the Princess Royal, Princess Michael of Kent and the Vice-Admiral Timothy Laurence exit Westminster Abbey, following the wedding ceremony.

However, there were also some Commonwealth leaders, members of religious organisations, diplomatic corps, military officials, members of the royal household, members of foreign royal families, representatives of charity and others whom Prince William worked with. All the close members of the royal family came to the wedding – including William's Uncles and Aunts, such as Prince Andrew, Princess Anne, Prince Edward and Viscount Linley. There were plenty of royal cousins, too, including the Duke and Duchess of Kent, the Earl and Countess of Ulster and Prince and Princess Michael of Kent. Members of Diana's family were also present, including Earl Spencer, William's Uncle. Kate, of course, had her close family there, as well as other relatives.

Among the celebrities invited were David and Victoria Beckham and film director, Guy Ritchie. Former English rugby coach, Sir Clive Woodward was there with his wife, Lady Woodward. Comedian Rowan Atkinson was also invited. The Middletons also invited the chairman of Reading Football Club, John Madejski, who was a personal friend. Mario Testino, the photographer who took Kate and William's engagement photos was also there. Of course, Kate and William like any other couple had their childhood friends and school and university friends there, as well, to celebrate the day together.

The night before the wedding, hundreds of people lined the streets of London, hoping they'd be the lucky enough to catch a glimpse of Kate and William on their big day. At every point along the route, behind the barricades, people gathered. With hours to go, the crowd camped outside Clarence House got a right, royal surprise, as Prince William emerged to chat to the crowds and accept good wishes. Looking relaxed and dressed casually, William shook hands and posed for photos. The visit heightened the sense of party that was already beginning to invade the capital. Earlier in the day, well-wishers had spotted Kate and Prince Harry at a final run-through at Westminster Abbey, too. Such a prestigious event needed high security, which was why more than 1,500 soldiers, sailors and air crew were on duty

Prince William and Prince Harry greet guests prior to the royal wedding.

*British Prime Minister David Cameron and wife Samantha
arrive at Westminster Abbey ahead of the royal wedding.*

along the royal procession route, stretching for about a mile between Buckingham Palace and Westminster Abbey. There were also around 5,000 police, uniformed and undercover, on operation for the day. By first light, on April 29th, more and more bystanders, adorned in face paint, carrying Union Jack flags or wearing crazy hats or wedding gear, began to turn up. Flags worn as capes were a particular favourite. And the party wasn't just for the wedding guests. Crowds brought their own food and drinks, struck up conversations with strangers next to them, burst into song and provided their own entertainment, as they waited for the historic event to unfold. Elsewhere bets were being taken on the colour of the Queen's hat (it was yellow, with odds of 10/11).

Once the service in the Abbey had started, it was piped via loud speakers along the route, so that everyone heard the vows. When it came to the hymns, many of the crowd joined in, too, as they did with the final rendition of 'God Save the Queen.' Now it was time to see the royal couple as they went past in their open carriage. Naturally there was cheering and flag-waving and hand-clapping and a rush to see the famous kiss on the balcony.

Catherine, Duchess of Cambridge and Prince William,
Duke of Cambridge kiss on the balcony at Buckingham
Palace on April 29, 2011 in London, England.

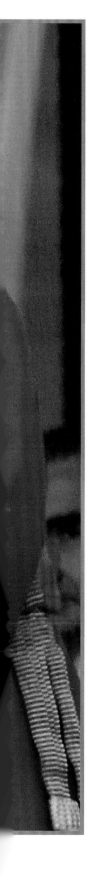

The Duke and Duchess of Cambridge approach Buckingham Palace by carriage procession, following their wedding.

Street Support

Kate and William returned from the Abbey in a carriage procession through Parliament Square, Whitehall, Horse Guards Parade and The Mall, waving to ecstatic crowds as they went. Around half a million people surrounded the Mall, waiting for the moment when the royal couple would hopefully emerge – and kiss – on the palace balcony. Once the couple arrived at Buckingham Palace after midday, they came out onto the balcony, followed by members of both families. To ecstatic cheering from the crowds below, Kate and William kissed not just once, but twice. 'I love you,' Prince William is reported to have said, adding 'let's give them another one.' As the families stood on the balcony, there was a fly-past by the Battle of Britain Memorial Flight of Lancaster, Spitfire and Hurricane planes, followed by two fighter jets and two tornados. It was so spectacularly noisy, that one of the young bridesmaids had to put her hands over her ears!

A general view of the Mall and Victoria Memorial filled with well-wishers celebrating the royal wedding.

Police officers stand in front of royal supporters on The Mall in London, along the processional route, in central London.

Ceremony

K ate and William chose a traditional Anglican wedding service. The Archbishop of Canterbury celebrated the marriage as the Church of England's most senior bishop. Richard Chartres, Bishop of London, preached the sermon. The service itself began with the procession of the Queen, Prince Philip and the clergy. Shortly afterwards, Kate Middleton arrived with her maid of honour, Pippa and her bridesmaids and pageboys. As the choir sang an anthem by Sir Hubert Parry, the bride made her three and a half minute procession from the Abbey doors to the altar on the arm of her father.

The service then proceeded with the formal service and congregational singing of three well-known hymns, along with fanfare, anthems, organ and orchestral music. The hymns chosen by Kate and William were 'Jerusalem', a famous hymn with words by British poet William Blake; 'Guide me O thou great redeemer', which is also the welsh rugby anthem (William is the vice-royal patron of the Welsh rugby union) the hymn was also sung at Diana's funeral; and another popular hymn by Charles Wesley, 'Love divine, all loves excelling.' The last hymn was also sung at the wedding of Prince Charles and Camilla Parker-Bowles in 2005. In their marriage vows, Kate and William promised to 'love, comfort, honour and keep' each other. They sealed their vows by exchanging a single ring, handed over by Prince Harry, as best man to the groom.

Prince William puts the ring on Kate, the Duchess of Cambridge's finger during their wedding ceremony.

Prince William and Kate exchange vows during their wedding ceremony.

The Bishop of London, Richard Chartres, opened his sermon with a quote from Catherine of Siena, a famous medieval Christian, whose feast day it was and who shared her name with the bride. The bishop urged Kate and William to live selflessly, remembering the needs of each other and aiming to transform each other with love. Chartres ended the sermon with a prayer created by Kate and William themselves. He read – 'God our Father, we thank you for our families; for the love that we share and for the joy of our marriage. In the busyness of each day, keep our eyes fixed on what is real and important in life and help us to be generous with our time and love and energy. Strengthened by our union, help us to serve and comfort those who suffer. We ask this in the Spirit of Jesus Christ. Amen.' The service then continued with prayers from the Dean and Archbishop. The choir also sang a newly composed choral anthem. After signing the registers, Kate and William walked down the aisle together, pausing to bow and courtesy to the Queen. The rest of their families and bridal party followed them down the aisle, including Kate's parents. As they left Westminster Abbey a peal of bells rang out across London. Kate and William passed through a guard of honour and were greeted with loud cheers from the waiting crowds. The marriage service was complete and William and Kate were now officially married!

Kate Middleton with her father, Michael Middleton arriving to attend her wedding to Prince William.

Kate Middleton with her father Michael at Westminster Abbey, followed by her sister Pippa Middleton.

Prince William and Kate make their way out of Westminster Abbey followed by Pippa Middleton, Prince Harry, Prince Charles, Carole Middleton, The Duchess of Cornwall and Michael Middleton.

Prince William exchanging vows with Kate.

Prince William, Duke of Cambridge and Catherine, Duchess of Cambridge leaving Westminster Abbey following their marriage ceremony, on April 29, 2011 in London, England.

Luncheon Reception

The eight tiered wedding cake made by Fiona Cairns and her team.

The Duke and Duchess of Cambridge driving from Buckingham Palace to Clarence House in a decorated vintage Aston Martin sports car.

Immediately after the wedding ceremony – or, more precisely, immediately after the kissing scene on the balcony – the Queen hosted a luncheon reception at Buckingham Palace for around 600 guests. Instead of an elaborate multi-course menu, Queen Elizabeth II chose finger foods to be served. Although Kate and William had full details of the luncheon, it was mainly overseen by the Queen. Approximately 10,000 canapes were prepared for the event by a team of 21 chefs, led by Royal Chef Mark Flanagan.

Guests were offered Pol Roger NV Brut Reserve Champagne to drink. All the ingredients for the canapés were sourced from companies that hold a royal warrant.

Guests at the luncheon were also present to see the traditional cutting of the cake. Kate and William had asked Fiona Cairns from Leicestershire to design the cake, which was a multi-tiered traditional fruit cake. The cake was decorated with cream and white icing and flowers such as those found on Kate's wedding dress (rose, thistle, daffodil and shamrock). Fiona Cairns started her business 25 years ago from her own kitchen table, Now she makes cakes that sell to Harrods, Selfridges and Waitrose. In the early 1980s Fiona left her job in graphics and became a pastry chef at a Michelin-starred restaurant. One Christmas she made some miniature cakes as gifts - her recipients were so impressed, they encouraged her to start her own business – and look where she is today!

The Duchess of Cambridge at Buckingham Palace after her wedding to Prince William.

*The Duchess of Cambridge leaving Clarence House to travel
to Buckingham Palace for the evening wedding celebrations.*

After Party

For the night-time party, there were fireworks, a live band led by popstar Ellie Goulding and Buckingham Palace's Throne Room was transformed into a massive nightclub. Only 300 people – the elite few closest family and friends – were invited to the do. Guests arrived at the pre-dinner drinks reception via a candle-lit walkway in the Palace courtyard, where bagpipers welcomed them. They were served vintage pink Champagne, peach bellinis and elderflower cocktails.

Each guest had been given an envelope with their table name on it. Tables were named after places that were meaningful to William and Kate, including places such as 'Lewa', after Lewa Downs in Kenya and 'Tetbury', a town in Gloucester close to Highgrove. There was also a 'St Andrews' table. Tables were a mix of royals, family and friends. Anton Mosimann, owner of Mosimann's private dining club in Belgravia, created the evening reception menu.

Wine came from the cellars of Buckingham Palace and Clarence House. The meal lasted about two hours. After everyone had eaten, Prince Harry stood up to deliver his speech. Prince Harry's typical best man speech had everyone in fits of laughter. Harry then introduced Kate's Dad, Michael, who gave his speech as father of the bride. He talked about the couple and about Kate's childhood. Michael also mentioned the day Prince William landed a helicopter in his garden on a visit to Kate and how it nearly blew the roof off his house! Prince William then made a speech thanking his father for hosting the party, offering the traditional toasts and commenting on his 'beautiful bride.'

As well as a dance-floor, there was a cocktail bar serving Champagne, spirits and Mojito cocktails. Ellie Goulding, a Brit award winner, delivered a live, two-hour set and then a mix of other songs. The final, official dance was 'She Loves You' by the Beatles. William and Kate, with their friends and families, then made their way to the palace gardens, where they were treated to a 3am firework display. Everyone declared it a magical, romantic end to a perfect day.

The Duchess of Cambridge attending a session of Youth
Parliament at the Legislative Assembly on July 5, 2011.

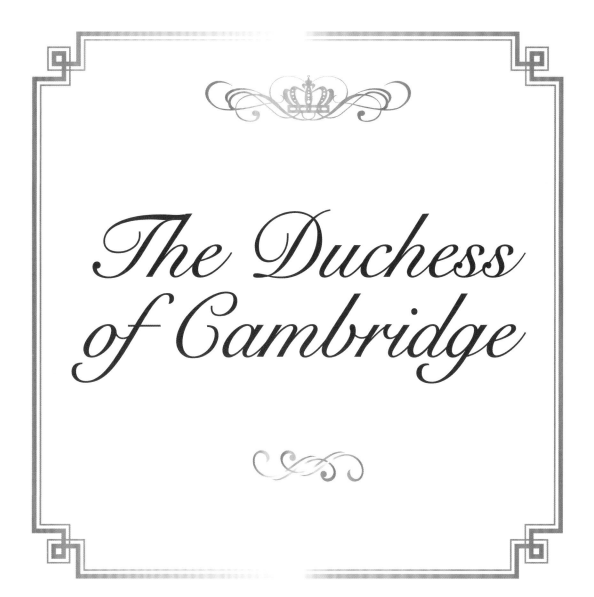

The Duchess
of Cambridge

The Duchess of Cambridge

Part of Kate's job as the Duchess of Cambridge is to support the Queen at home and overseas. This usually includes a number of public engagements and royal tours. As well as going with William, Kate carries out business with other members of the Royal family, like William's grandparents, the Queen and the Duke of Edinburgh, and her in-laws, Prince Charles and Camilla. She's also the royal patron of a number of organisations.

Kate had already been introduced to public appearances before she and William were married. In 2011, Kate officially named a life-boat stationed in North Wales and a day later she and William returned to St Andrews University to celebrate its 600th anniversary of its founding.

Although it can seem formal, Kate does get a say in what she does. Since becoming the Duchess of Cambridge, she's been able to take on charities and causes that are close to her own heart. Kate is currently patron of the National Portrait Gallery, The Art Room, Action on Addiction and East Anglia Children's Hospice. In fact, in her fist year as official Duchess of Cambridge and patron, she visited all four projects.

Kate Middleton, fiancée of Britain's Prince William, waves to members of the public during a visit to the University of St Andrews in Scotland, on February 25, 2011.

*The Duchess of Cambridge attending a dinner in aid of
the University of St Andrews 600th Anniversary Appeal.*

The Duke and Duchess of Cambridge speaking with British artist Paul Emsley after viewing his portrait of the duchess at the National Portrait Gallery in central London on January 11, 2013

It's clear that Kate's interest in art is one of the reasons she's chosen the National Portrait Gallery and the Art Room as organisations to be patron of. The National Portrait Gallery houses the nation's collection of portraits of important and famous British people and portraiture done by famous artists. It was the first portrait gallery in the world when it opened in 1856 in central London and is open to the public. The National Gallery also commissioned artist Nicky Philipps to paint a double portrait of Princes William and Harry, which went on show for the first time in 2010. Kate's first official portrait by Paul Emsley also hangs in the National Portrait Gallery, as well as several other portraits of Royal Family members. The Art Room is a National Portrait Gallery project. It helps school children - largely in deprived areas - to increase their self-esteem, self-confidence and independence through drawing, painting and modelling. Three months after getting married, Kate took off on her first official overseas visit on behalf of the Queen with William.

Paul Emsley poses in front of his portrait of Catherine.
The Duchess of Cambridge after its unveiling.

The pair visited Canada and North America on an 11-day tour. It was said that the Queen, who is very fond of her son's wife, invited Kate to choose from her extensive collection of exquisite jewellery for the trip. As Canada is a commonwealth country, the Queen is still sovereign there. Kate and William touched down in Ottawa in a Canadian air forces jet, which they'd left Heathrow in. Kate even managed a change of clothing! As part of the tour, they greeted the crowds of well-wishers, as well as attending special events and meeting Canadian VIPS, such as the Canada Prime Minister and his wife and the Governor General, who is the Queen's representative in Canada. But it wasn't all formal occasions – Kate and William also took part in a fun dragon boat race and went to the world's richest rodeo at the Calgary Stampede. They also attended a centre for at-risk youth and spent the night on a warship.

At the end of their nine-day tour of Canada, Kate and William added a quick visit to Los Angeles. They were there to do some fundraising and to promote American investment in the UK and charitable work, including visiting a technology summit in Beverley Hills, which was aimed at promoting American investment in British tech companies.

Catherine, Duchess of Cambridge participates in a ceramics class during a visit to Inner City Arts on July 10, 2011 in Los Angeles, California.

*The Duke and Duchess of
Cambridge and Catherine
departing LAX airport on a British
Airways scheduled flight on July
10, 2011 in Los Angeles, California.*

*The Duke And Duchess of Cambridge watching the
Calgary Stampede Parade, in Calgary, Alberta.*

143

At the beginning of 2012, Kate announced that she would become a volunteer for the National Scouting Association. She was inspired by her love of the outdoor and love of young people. The following year, Kate was present at The National Review of Queen's Scouts at Windsor Castle. This is an event that celebrates outstanding achievements from individual scouts and is the highest award they can achieve.

The second overseas trip Kate and William took was to Malaysia, Singapore, the Solomon Islands and Tuvalu as part of Her Majesty The Queen's Jubilee year celebrations. Highlights included visiting a mosque in the centre of Kuala Lumpur, which is the biggest in Malaysia, able to host 12,000 people; meeting the celebrated and

Catherine, Duchess of Cambridge attending the National Review of Queen's Scouts, at Windsor Castle on April 21, 2013.

The Duke and Duchess of Cambridge wave in Tuvalu in Funafuti on September 19, 2012.

Malaysia-born shoe designer, Jimmy Choo, at a British-style tea party; and dancing in grass skirts at a traditional welcome dance on the South Pacific island of Tuvalu. This was a momentous year for Britain as a whole. As well as the Queen's Jubilee, it was the year the Olympics came to London and when sport-fever gripped the capital. The Duke and Duchess of Cambridge, both keen sports people at school and University, were official ambassadors for Team GB and Paralympic GB.

And if that wasn't enough, at the end of 2012 in December, Kate and William had a final special announcement to make: they were expecting their first baby - a future King or Queen of Britain. What a year for the Duchess of Cambridge!

145

The Duchess of Cambridge outside King Edward VII Hospital in London.

The Baby

Royal Baby

On the 3rd December 2012, St James' Palace announced that the Duchess of Cambridge was pregnant with her first child. The announcement was made earlier than usual – about eight weeks into the pregnancy – because Kate had been admitted into the King Edward VII hospital in London, suffering from severe morning sickness (hyperemesis gravidarum). She stayed in hospital for three days. The couple had been hoping to keep the exciting news to themselves until after the usual 12 week scan and had initially planned on announcing their baby news at Sandringham during the Christmas holidays.

After a short stay in hospital, where Kate's condition stabilised (one in 50 women suffer from acute morning sickness at some stage in their pregnancy, which can involve vomiting and dehydration), Kate was allowed home and advised to rest. Kate and William both said they were 'immensely grateful' for all the support and good wishes the public had shown them during this time.

After Christmas, on January 14th 2013, St James' Palace announced that Kate and William's baby was expected to be born in July 2013. At the same time, the Queen issued new letters patent that said all children of the eldest Prince of Wales would be able to have the title 'Royal Highness', instead of just the oldest, as had been traditional up until then.

Kate leaves hospital after a 4 day stay due to acute morning sickness.

Prince William and Kate prepare to leave hospital.

Just a couple of months later, there was a rumour that Kate had unwittingly let slip the gender of her and William's first-born. On a visit to Grimbsy, one well-wisher had handed the Duchess a teddy bear, when Kate is reported to have said, 'I'll take that for my d-' before stopping herself. Spectators insist that she was about to say 'daughter', but Kate remained firmly, and politely, tight-lipped after that and any royal communication on the subject was at pains to stress that the royal couple had no idea whether they were expecting a boy or a girl.

Rumours were also rife about baby names, with leading bookmakers offering odds before the birth on everything from Alexandra, Elizabeth, Diana and Victoria to George, Philip, James and John.

Kate attends The Willows Primary School, Wythenshawe to launch a new school counselling program.

*The Duchess Of Cambridge is presented
with flowers on a visit to Naomi House.*

One thing was certain – Kate and William had decided that, with
all being well and going to plan, Kate would give birth at St Mary's
Hospital in Paddington – the same hospital where William and his
brother Harry had been born. The doctors they chose to look after
Kate's pregnancy and birth were Marcus Setchell, the Queen's doctor
for over 20 years and Alan Farthing, a Harley Street doctor, who has
been an obstetrician and gynaecologist to the Queen since 2008 and
consultant at St Mary's.

Kate's Pregnancy Outfits

K ate made her first post-pregnancy appearance on the steps outside the hospital where she'd been treated for acute morning sickness. She wore a dark blue Diane von Furstenberg coat and a pretty lilac pashmina-scarf. Despite her sickness, she looked radiant, clasping a bunch of yellow flowers and smiling at the side of her husband, Prince William.

On a trip to Grimsby, where she crouched down on black high heels to accept flowers from little children, Kate wore a chocolate-brown Hobbs Celeste coast with a dress from Great Plains. She's been seen in the coat before - it's clearly one of her flattering favourites.

For a charity visit with Prince William, Kate chose a black dress from high street chain, Topshop and managed to look chic and elegant. It was back to designer-wear for a visit to the Underground with the Queen – she wore a blue coat by Malene Birger, onto which she'd pinned a cute 'baby on board' badge. As her due date neared, Kate started to choose a range of bespoke maternity wear, including a stunning pale blue empire-line dress, by British designer Emilia Wickstead, which she wore for an event at the National Portrait Gallery.

Throughout her pregnancy, Kate managed to show that you could still be style-savvy, chic and elegant, no matter how big or small your bump. Pregnant women everywhere were watching – and as usual copying – Kate's iconic style.

Kate makes an official visit to Baker Street Underground Station.

Kate receives a posy of flowers as she visits the National Fishing Heritage Centre.

*Kate attends an evening reception to celebrate the
work of the charity at the National Portrait Gallery.*

Kate carries her new-born son as she and Prince William leave
The Lindo Wing at St Mary's Hospital on July 23rd, 2013.

Prince George Alexander Louis, first son of the Duke and Duchess of Cambridge, was born on Monday 22nd July 2013 at 4.24pm. The third in line to the throne was welcomed into the world weighing a healthy 8lbs 6oz at St Mary's Hospital, Paddington, London.

The Duchess had been admitted to hospital from Kensington Palace in the 'early stages of labour' and was accompanied by the Duke at 6am on Monday 22nd July 2013. A team of royal protection officers rushed the mother-to-be into the hospital via a rear exit, the same route taken by Princess Diana when she gave birth to William in 1982.

After the baby was born later the same day, the couple requested some privacy. They called family to tell them the news, but it wasn't until 8.29pm that the news was broken to the public – four hours after the birth. Royal protocol is such that a gilded easel, holding an A4 piece of paper is placed outside Buckingham Palace with the birth announcement and signatures. The message read simply:

'Her Royal Highness The Duchess of Cambridge was safely delivered of a son at 4.24 p.m. The baby weighs 8 pounds 6 ounces. Her Royal Highness and her child are both doing well.'

The first sign of a royal wave from baby George.

*Kate passes the baby to
Prince William.*

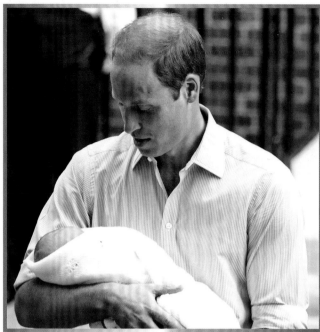

*Prince William answers questions from the press and
jokes that the baby has Kate's looks.*

The next day, the royal prince had his first family visitors. Michael and
Carole Middleton arrived at 3pm at the hospital in a taxi. Emerging
from the Lindo Wing a while later, they approached waiting crowds
to answer a few questions. 'He's absolutely beautiful,' said Carole.
'They're both doing really well and we're so thrilled.' At 5.30pm the
other set of grandparents arrived – Charles and Camilla – looking
equally happy.

There were gun salutes in Green Park, Westminster Abbey rang its
bells for three hours and crowds gathered to photograph the easel that
held the momentous news outside the gates of Buckingham Palace.
Finally the public was given its first glimpse of the new royal. The
Duke and Duchess of Cambridge, smiling widely, introduced their
baby boy to crowds and the world's media outside St Mary's hospital,
Paddington at 7.15pm on July 23rd.

Both the Duke and Duchess agreed that it had been 'an emotional
time, a special time, something that any parent can relate to.' Soon
after his first public appearance, the new prince emerged from the
hospital, carried by his father in a very modern car-seat. William then
drove his family to Kensington Palace. The Queen and Prince Harry
also met the newest member of the royal family for the first time.

Two days after the birth, it was announced that the baby had been
named George Alexander Louis. The young royal will be known
as HRH Prince George of Cambridge – and as King George VII,
when he becomes monarch. Prince George spent his first night at
Kensington Palace, before heading off with the Duke and Duchess to
his grandparents' estate in Bucklebury, Berkshire.

*Kate and William pose for photographs before heading
to Kensington Palace with their new-born.*

A glowing Kate holding baby George outside St Mary's Hospital.